For my beloved Oskar
—Britta

Text by Patricia Hegarty • Text copyright © 2017 by Little Tiger Press • Cover art and interior illustrations copyright © 2017 by Britta Teckentrup
All rights reserved. Published in the United States by Doubleday, an imprint of Random House Children's Books, a division of Penguin Random House
LLC, New York. Originally published in the United Kingdom by Little Tiger Press in 2017. • Doubleday and the colophon are registered trademarks
of Penguin Random House LLC. • Library of Congress Cataloging-in-Publication Data is available upon request. ISBN 978-1-5247-6966-6 (trade) •
MANUFACTURED IN CHINA • 10 9 8 7 6 • First American Edition • Random House Children's Books supports the First Amendment and

MOON

A Peek-Through
Picture Book

Illustrated by
Britta Teckentrup

Have you ever wondered why
The moon shines in the nighttime sky?

How every creature, plant, and tree
Is subject to its mystery?

A breeze blows softly across the land,
Rippling through the desert sand.

A scorpion scuttles through the night,
Glowing with an eerie light.

Far away, in a land harsh and bare,
Puffins shiver in the cold night air.

The northern lights set the skies aglow,
Shimmering, glimmering, above the snow.

As birds fly south to warmer climes,
They seem to sense the perfect time.

Shining strongly through the night,
The moon will always guide their flight.

In the jungle, through the green,
Shafts of silvery light are seen.

As parrots swoop beneath the moon,
Tree frogs croak their nightly tune.

On southern shores, on a moonlit night,
Nature reveals a magical sight.

Hundreds of turtles swim to land
To lay their eggs in the soft white sand.

When nights are dark and the moon is new,
A tiny field mouse has work to do.

Busily scampering here and there,
It hunts for food in the cool night air.

The ocean sparkles, bluey-green,
Lit up by a magical scene.

Waves roll gently to and fro.
The moon commands their ebb and flow.

Above the mountainside at night,
The sky is filled with sparkling light.

As wispy clouds scutter by,
A shining moonbow lights the sky.

In the grassland, all is still.
Animals rest in the nighttime chill.

After a day of blazing heat,
The cool, clear air smells fresh and sweet.

Snowflakes fall on frozen ground.
Swirling, twirling, they make no sound.

Under the moon, huddled together,
Penguins seek warmth in the icy weather.

So, when you close your eyes at night,
Imagine the moon's twinkling light,

Shining down with a silvery glow
As we dream our dreams in the world below.